FRANÉ LESSAC

Australia Under the Sea

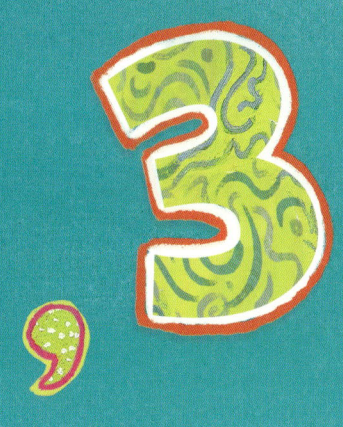

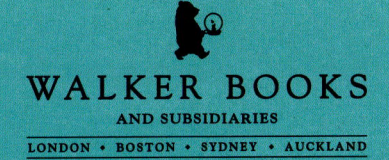

1, 2, 3

WALKER BOOKS
AND SUBSIDIARIES
LONDON · BOSTON · SYDNEY · AUCKLAND

Coral is alive. It is made up of thousands of tiny animals.

When lots of corals grow close together, it is called a reef.

Many amazing creatures make their homes on a coral reef.

Whale sharks are the largest fish in the sea but they eat the smallest of plants and animals.

Some whale sharks can grow as long as a bus!

Dugongs love to graze on seagrass.
That's why some people call them sea cows.

3 Three playful clownfish…

4 Four clever dolphins...

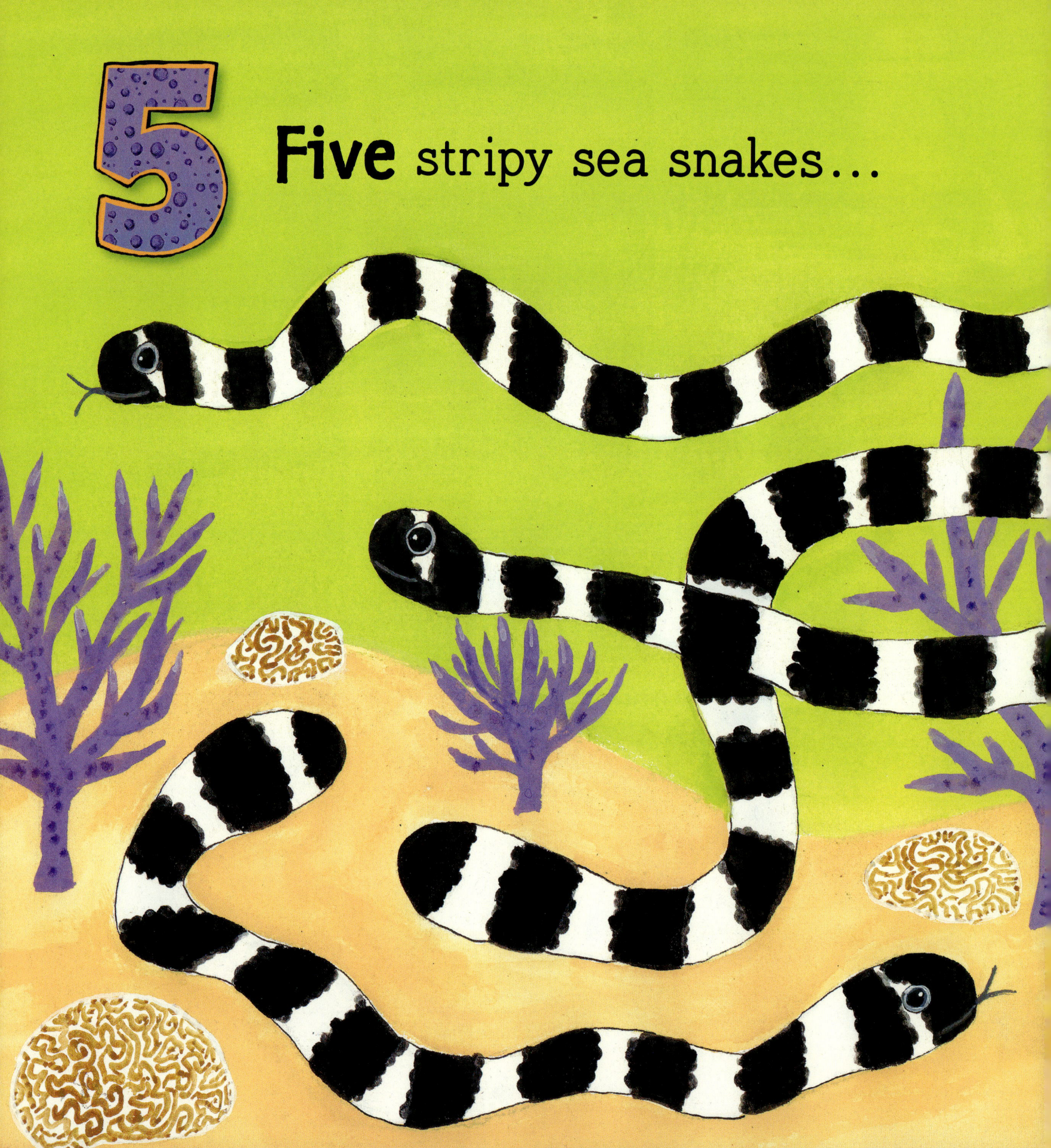

 **Six** hungry turtles...

Green turtles always eat their vegetables – seaweed and sea lettuce.

They are one of the world's largest sea turtles.

7 Seven busy parrotfish...

8 **Eight** spotted rays...

When rays swim, they look like birds flapping their wings.

Eagle rays have poisonous spines on their long, thin tails.

 **Nine** wobbly jellyfish...

Jellyfish are not fish.
They are sea creatures mostly made up of water.

Moon jellyfish look a lot like floating moons.

10 **Ten** blue sea stars...

Sea stars use their hundreds of tiny tube-like feet to move around.

When a sea star loses an arm, it can grow a new one. That's handy!

11 Eleven snappy crabs...

Crabs have ten legs. The front two are called claws and are used to grab things. The other eight are used for walking.

Seahorses wrap their tails around sponges, coral or sea plants to stop from floating away.

Seahorses will never win a race. They are one of the slowest fish in the ocean.

Coral reefs are important because they keep the sea healthy.

A healthy reef means a healthy sea.
A healthy sea means a healthy planet.